The Glass Book

for Martin
the trumpetist
with heartfelt respect

La poesia se ha portado bien
Yo me portado horriblemente mal
                    Nicanor Parra

the glass book
Poems

tim lander

Ekstasis Editions

Canadian Cataloguing in Publication Data

Lander, Tim, 1938-
      The glass book (poems)

      Poems
      ISBN 1-896860-62-1

         I. Title.
      Ps8573.A535G6   1999   C811'.54   C99-911104-3
      PR9199.3.L362G5   1999

Cover Photo: Connie Fife

Acknowledgements:
Most of these poems have previously appeared as copy-free chapbooks.
The Myth of Adam and Eve was published in a hand-printed edition by
Rusty North at Sagitarrius Press, Port Townsend, Washington. If you
make use of any of these poems, please let us know.
lander_tim@hotmail.com.

Published in 1999 by:
Ekstasis Editions Canada Ltd.   Ekstasis Editions
Box 8474, Main Postal Outlet   Box 571
Victoria, B.C. V8W 3S1   Banff, Alberta T0L 0C0

The Canada Council | Le Conseil des Arts
for the Arts | du Canada
since 1957 | depuis 1957

The Glass Book has been published with the assistance of a grant from the
Canada Council and the Cultural Services Branch of British Columbia.
Do not reproduce without love.

Contents

Who will tell secrets
of the old sky
worn full of holes
patched by stars
woven with birds
and mocked by men?

A fellow came
robbed heaven of its laughter
and wrapped it round his face
he took the sorrow too
and tied that on his feet
ran off through the snow
in a flat land
full of knife edged dreams
following a frozen river
to the sea

Nanaimo elegy
for Joshua McGrail

If an elegant
 though maybe impoverished
 aristocrat
  of either sex
would lend me her castle
 in the mountains
I'm sure the Muse
 (or Orpheus)
  would bend down
   and stroke my hair;
but in this coffee shop
 if I cry out
  who would hear me
   among these grumbling souls?
and if I cry out
 who would take care of my dog
  who sits outside in the bushes
while the security guards
 call the police
  to gently conduct me
to the psychiatric ward for observation?

Shades of Poetry in Tartarus
 have pity on me!
With bent nails and knotty two by fours
 scrounged from demolished buildings
  I'm erecting a ladder up to Heaven

I haven't reached the tree tops yet
 and before I meet my first angel
  it's sure to be condemned by City Hall
   for contravention of a bilaw against overreaching
   or as a hazard to aeronautical navigation
So much for Hubris
So much for my wooden Babel

Well no
 this ain't no Duino
  but I am blessed
   here in Nanaimo
Outside the mall
 the sun is shining
  and every year is a milestone
   marked by poets that I've managed to outlive
and if I can just keep writing
 maybe I can gain
  some notoriety
even though my music is thin
 my cadence weak
  and my spelling worst of all

Here I am
 you young flames of poetry!
Imagine the mirage
 of wisdom in grey hair
  my toothless smile
but if you can find any wisdom here
 it is your own
the words you thought you heard me say or sing
 are really psychobabble
  echoed in your inner ear
Do not neglect the echoing
 in your inner ear

But to get back to Duino
 Who's knocking on the castle door?

Hey, Let's not
 get caught up
  in that old Scotch tragedy
but castles are not castles
 for nothing
they're the unassailable presence of power
 among the population.

To sit in an age old fortress
 and write poetry
  at the bloody and brutal
   intersections of history
swaggering heros,
 deserted aristocratic ladies
  and men at arms who go out
   rape and slaughter
   and die horribly
hacked to death
 spilling their guts on some battle field
  or enjoying a slow agony
   stinking of gangrene

and the world turns
 and the world is all the same
  the song of hope
   and the song of lamentation.

When I cry out
 who among the angels
  would take time out
   to humour me?

but the angels are all busy somewhere else
 or are they all asleep?
  or moonlighting in Disneyland

and today is now
 and history

    —1996

POEM FOR THE ONE EYED CARPENTER
for Ronny Walker, and the Clam Diggers of Nanaimo

The myth of old men
 the doom of ages
  withered thighs

and ancient cocksure animals
 grey souls
  withered hopes and expectations

and the way you danced
 all summer once
  while the trees were full of stars

and the lie you told me
 the cry of the heron
  in the deepening twilight

and now you mutter to me
 those petty unfolding histories

and always on the bridge
 between life and death
pissing over the parapet
 into the rushing stream.

"And the river of life" you said
 "you can jump in once
you cannot test it with your toe

 it gives no second chance
as you are swept
 on a wild ride downstream.

"Go with the current
 go where the water flows deepest
  and fastest

do not turn aside
 or you'll be caught
  in eddies and whirlpools

snagged and dragged under
 by logjams
  the drowned branches
  of washed out trees

at last thrown lifeless
 on the unwelcoming bank
  of another spring.

"Take the fastest flow of the river
 fix your eye unflinchingly
  on the way you must go.

"Learn the song of the river, its dance
 the gossip of small birds
  and the little creatures
   that burrow in the banks

the legends of proud fish
 keeping station in the rapids."

"Then", you say "These purposes
 What?" you say "These purposes?
  These idle ideal purposes"

Those histories
 we'll write those histories
they are your histories
 the histories of people

Clamdiggers to the sand bar
 women and children
bent in the cold dark night
 raking at the gravel bank
  picking with frozen fingers
   among the small stones.

Herring skiffs by sea lanes
 and rocks of the night,
  wheel and pitch and plunge about
   You found a prayer
    on the lips of night
for the false way we know
 the secret falsity of the ocean
  among the grinding rocks

the terrible swirling darkness
 of the ocean
  that leaps up to heaven
   and down again
into the pit of the waves
 till the waves become a world about us
and bear us again skywards.

Do you remember how dark the sea is
 how cold and grey it might become?

 mixt as it is with our blood
  with our fathers' blood
and our mothers' sac of water

 with the memories of moving waters
and the cry of the seabird
 the cold cry that transfixes memory

the oily rising flotsam at the tide's edge
 the careless artifacts of human life
  among the sea wrack
   and the world of crabs

and so we set out
 to discover history
  among all the broken bottles
   and sand dunes of the world

"It's night" you say
 the colours of the world are deepening
  but still the trees cry out
   "we are still green"
    into the teeth
of the rising dark

and we wonder
 in this world
  where everything has become a metaphor
   for the path we are forcing on the world
for the path we insist
 that all of life must follow

no shining path this one
 but a path through smoke
  and the gathering gloom
by ruined fields
 and poisoned gardens

This is the way
 we've decided we must tread
we have drawn a blue print
 built a prototype of hell.

Oh Jesus! You poor carpenter
 little did you know!

—1991

And to the end of it
we seemed how much inside it all
    with light
You are a creature of such teeth
and you have set them in a hive of radiance
  You glimmer with the darkness of the times
It's dangerous to be about these days
  but you have crept
    by inches and by eons
    out of the swamp
      of shared mortality
You come with a tooth in your head
and a little glint in your eye
and clay matting your hair
  You came, you see
    among the rushes
      and mating frogs
        it was that season
Looking a little like a grey old man
or someones memory from undersea
and the rock pool handed you
  a broken water crown
    a voice sprang up
      and moved out of your mouth
telling the birds
  as though perhaps they did not know
how brilliant the sun
cold clear   was water
  and how blue
    or looked so close
  the mountains over there
Beyond the bay, and farther shoreline
  with its cedars
You seem to be a thing of water
whistling aqueously
  as you plan a slow return
    towards the creeks jewel pebbles
    and swaying water grass

Travellers

for Elaine Briere

I

And so much dreaming
 must be worth while
a knife full of pain
 a song remembering early love
and the wind
 that leaps out of the past
straight through the eye
 into the chambers
 of a mortgaged heart

"Back to adolescence!" you say
 and the flat air
Lay beside me again, sweet bodies
 Towards the viciousness of middle age
this age is crackling within us
 also tonight
 but then it's growing huge
 in all our bones
 as well

Nanaimo, where the ferries come
 and go
Departure Bay and Duke Point
 Petroglyph Park
 and the quick running deer

Give the treasure of our hearts
 the knowledgeable gift
 the gift of silence

Oh weep, weep
 in this delirium
 we've wandered so deep
Love bird, love bird

give me a sparkling word
 sing me a song
  so wide, so strong

Would you call this
 our pleasurable land?
This the land of our flowing out
the territory of our silent shout
 once the land of the open hand
  the depths of sorrow
   where we stand
chinful in history
 chinful in dry stumps
  rattled ghosts, rusty chains
and broken logging engines

you close the book on us
 brimful of darkness

Willingly, as you might say
or willfully, as the case might be
and deceitfully, you see
and this you gave to me
a songbird on a distant tree
 in a honeyed land
  beyond the sea
or a tattered coat
 on a broken branch
  on a gravel spit
   by a wasted shore
and all these things
 and the faintest shadows of them
  fly from your sharpened voice
   that you carry around
   with incredible noise
like the yelling of angels
 in god's backyard place
  as they play at volley ball
   in the eternal coffee break
    between those moments of creation

16

No way back
  to the faded shore
  and the song of the man
  who walked on the rocks
  whistled into the harsh salt wind
  as he searched for remnants
  of fishermens' lies
  and rumours of wars
  among the barnacles
  and the grinding of teeth
  in the faces of clocks

You must be sure of something
  as you place the cigaret
between y'r teeth

II

Parzival, you've ridden far
  in your rusty armour
   with a question in your knapsack
   and a piece of hard grey bread
Your socks have known no needles
  since they left your mother's salty care
and the cold hard earth, your nightfall
  a faithful inducer of significant dreams

That fortress, once you found so easily
  dissolved in November
  somewhere beyond the mist,
and as you know
  you got to turn the wheel of time y'rself
  to reclaim some April
   from under an eroded stone
   where toads sleep.
And the uncomfortable memory
  of your mother's prayers
  and your father's explorations
of the lost continent of fog

are scratchings by twilight
 from the flakey scalp of history
eternal passages
 of wandering in peat bogs
  betrayed by lying compass needles
   metallic bodies
and hungry dancing Will o'Whisp.

But come April
 the rising sun
  burns holes in the ramparts of mist
flights of water-birds
 make of the marsh
 a gossipy nursery
and the hungry grin of winter
 turns to primrose summer
  watching the nests
   of bittern and mallard
    grow full, then ripe
  then fluffy, loud and hungry
at last to take to the waterway
 with the yellowing of rushes
  heat of summer
dragonflies and swallows
 gnat catching
  on the sky reflecting water.

But does the spring
 need that tender youth
  to find his imagined manhood
before it can burst
 like an over ripe puffball
to ensure the frenzy and buzz
 and stench of life again?

And that other traveller
 come high summer
the club footed boy
 from over the mountain
  with his dried fish

and his stout stick
for beating at bushes
and cracking rabbits' skulls
limping along
with a misconstrued oracle
humming its ragtime
in the coils of his ear?

You thought you knew
as in the darkness
of your ignorance
you stumbled on your father
among the sheep turds
in a dry pasture
and left his broken body
for the crows

Likewise your mother
in a different way
your children doomed
by family quarreling
two brothers at each others' throats
the turn of history, you say
limping out the drought
of your arid imagination.

So pluck words
from the mouth of the cunning
the world can still be grabbed
by trickery and hidden names,
and a little surprising violence
suddenly placed
bring down the whole damned mountain
on the apathetic heads
of human greed
You either know, or don't
and in your wisdom
negligent anger
grounds us all
in unending mockery

All these words are ancient tragedy
"Irrelevant," you say, "to our predicament"

"Real nice body on it
 real nice interior ..."
some guy bullshitting
 about his obsolete machine
one night in the Rendez-vous Cafe

    III

"The King is wounded in the groin"
 you tell me
and the undersecretary of the imagination
 stubbed his toe
  among the barnacles
   sea-wrack and hermit crabs
   and bitchy sea-gulls
hunting critters with his kid
 in the rock pools
  under a blue July sky

and the waitress in the coffee shop
 the one who always calls you "dear"
cut her thumb
 while slicing balony
  for samwiges, for samwiges, for samwiges
  she swore a bit
   sucked it once
    taped it up
and topped your coffee cup —

and the premier of somewhere disappeared
 in a puff of smoke
  on a May morning
   beyond the fourteenth tee
and this all our politics
 is thoroughly ashamed of us
  jubilantly electioneering

the jelly roll
 belly flop
of our civic responsibilities

You tell me then your lies
 in several independent languages
  and cryptograms that form themselves
  so powerfully on the edges
   of our culinary delight

Oh! Canada!
 my lovely one
it is of you I dream my nights
 "And did those feet in ancient times
 walk upon Cypress Hills?"
  you ask again
"and did a tragic history
 strut its stuff, unnoticed
 in the bright cold of our fields?"

Everything is open to interpretation
 all the doors are open
 all the windows
 all the competitions
 to places in the sun
 to the good life
 and tunnels of love as well

All are open
 to close with a clang
 fastened with locks
 and hands and eyes
an unpleasant surprise
and where did we leave the children?

If love is to flower
 if love is a flower
like the dream you told me of
 like the mouth
  that presses to my mouth

21

like the voice that goes out
  to find mine
  as I retract it, presently

and you met us
  in the midst of summer
Voyages to difficult islands
  desire under dusty trees
   and spaces where we flash
    in litanies of ardure
    and musky sorrow
old words that hide themselves
  in chemistries of flesh

"The King is wounded in the groin"
  you tell me
but we recognise each others' voices
  in the passing storm
"Sapiens, sapiens" we call each other
    "Sapiens"
So much like here
  the wisdom of the moment
  the knowledge of water
  as it runs
  or frozen too
  is more like us perhaps
  as we are grounded
   in these points of silence

Truthfully, you say so too
  too much it is
   for us as well
    the truth, I mean

How long we've waited
   in the silence too
   in the snow, in the rain
   in the traffic, cigaret smoke
in pubs and coffee houses
  and greyhound depots

and watched words
  being formed on inarticulate lips
and sat around
 hatching plots
  off washroom walls
   as well —
It's all quite right you see
 that's quite like us, you see

     IV

We the obscure
 the obese, the obscene
obesity of the spirit is what I mean
 and obscenity too, you know

the world is full of loving women
    glory be to god
    Glory be to God
the World is full of Loving WoMen

Have you known the King in his sorrow?
 the Kingdom of Sorrow
  is rich in words.

The Thief of Words
 is hiding in the vineyards
he pours our wine upon the pathways
 and sings as it soaks in our dusty footprints
he'll betray himself so deeply
 in his scurrilous song
  of the rich kelpy sea
   and the rain that beat
   on the hissing water

We'll hang him by his high kicking heels
 from a distant groaning tree
and when the sea is calm, or not
 you'll see him shining there

a lightening rod to any wandering gale
 on a further shore
  to that he walked upon
   those spring evenings
 whispering in the abstracted ear of love.

And the Thief of Time
 is out breaking bottles
  pouring the beer
   over his sweetheart's sweaty body
 watching it foam between her breasts
  over her round dimpled belly
laughing, tossing the empties
 at an old fig tree.

The Thief of Sunlight
 is away hunting butterflies
navigates the Amazon
 in a hollowed out tree trunk

he pulls off their wings
 and smokes up their corpses
  sells them to tourists
   as butterfly jerky

he also did the Volga
 and some say the Mackensie
  on inflatable rafts
   of bits of bovine guts

expanded to the ultimate
 with hyperbolic adjectives
  trying to keep them ship-shape
   amid the frothy seas of metaphor

he's taking a trip
 through our national geographic
  his name is measured mightily
   in Codak anthropology

baroquery and erotica
 carved in ancient limestone
among the lianas
 and spectacular biting spiders

the furry monsters
 that we love to haunt
our oh so teevee comfortable
 instant imagination

and the sacred serpents
 that lie in feign-ed sleep
  just above the heads
   of bare footed supplicants

this is his dream
 he loves it so completely

but termites are chewing
 at his waterlogged bato
  and pirhanas escort him
   harmoniously suck their gums

and African bees
 have scouted out his carcass
  aim to turn it into honey comb
   as the breath departs him

he's in quite dire circumstances
 but he hardly knows it
he sings himself a love song
 and whistles through his broken teeth.

And the Matriarch of Tears
 is the queen of bitter fruit
and laughter in the garden
 has circumscribed with rainbows
  all the paths of childhood
   from beyond the edge of memory

The Flood has returned
 the budget appropriations
  for Noah's Ark
   are incomplete

the keels laid
 and the skeleton
  sticks up into the rain clouds
while under skin umbrellas
 the carpenters are puffing grass

and the dripping animals
 wonder at the best made plans
  of gods and men
which have all gone astray
 in some celestial burocracy

and the blue prints ran right off the paper
 in the pelting rain.

The Ministry of Pain
 has stampt us once again
the Undersecretary of Agony
 thumbs a memo on salt and fire.

with virtuous patience
 the Gardener of Thorn Trees
  is fattening up the maggots
   to hatch them into deer flies

and send them humming homewards
 to that old haven of despair
  the ultimate ruin
   the cold hearts' refuge
   the inevitable nowhere

all that's left
 in this princedom of permafrost
  where the wind piles the snow seed.
      —1980

at this edge
and beyond us
a field of broken brick

and at our feet
the ants are marching
and in our shaking fist
a word we hurl at heaven

Supposing
so many poems
spoken with the voice of the
gun?

and supposing
the flowers of peace
bear the seeds
of deceit?

The Glass Book
for Jeniffer Franklin

"They say the cause of revolution
is hunger in interplanetary spaces.
We need to sow wheat out there, in the ether"
Osip Mandelstam

THE SECRET OF IT ALL
is the return from the grave
the way you came back
visiting us in the old house
after so many hours or years of sleep

The secret of it all
was the way you slipped through the door
with your eyes and your voice
with the silence burning at your lips
with your hands full of the dust of time
and the unlikely explanations we label survival
and histories told in bones and rags
the vanished spasm
that is the pride of us all

The secret of it all
the way we travel faster than fire
further than the best we can produce
out of sight with the teeth you bore then
the gritted teeth
the throat full of words
spitting phlegm and blood
that's so sweet to taste
falling as flowers to the ground
as heart shaped flowers
on the ripening ground
that gives the sun back a glance
that move the sun on a notch
into another spring

To the sudden remembrance of all those others
gone down the tunnel we are always emerging from
the unattainable light always at the end
our house always behind us in the fog we've departed

How like fugitives
we left the echoing rooms of memory
of the mind so full
of the sound of footsteps on the stairs
of footsteps of the beloved distancing on floors above
the slight sweet limp among the pattering feet
voices penetrating the walls
saturating the old dried wood
driving out termites and little birds

The voices of children echoing and echoing
years after the abandonment of this chilly mansion
the birth room and the death room
the windows opening on gardens full of the past
overgrown even in the days of childhood
and the child's mind so full
of the lingering fragrance of cotton dresses
shadowed on green lawns
frayed now and scattered

You've seen it all from your vantage point
you've been about and grown amazed
at the nature of man that binds us
in this historic cul de sac

We've seen the ocean of nothing
the city of sounds
the groaning dead city
of total indifference
we've had a bunch of knowledge
just like this
we collect it and arrange it
creating categories
so many details
and who's to impose a meaning?

Memories expelled denied avoided
faces empty of eyes
eyes gone away
the past picked up by the wind
that moves between heaven and the sea
that roars to the height of stupidity
that crashes on the rocks of intransigence
and all the eroded pits of memory
where we still feel the prick of embarrassment

Rank weeds in the garden
plunge their roots deep in the subsoil
you pull at them
they only snap
and grow again their crown of leaves
and in the trees
moss on the unpruned bough
and echoes of children
laughing down the apples
the discarded toy
discovered by the gardener
as he turns his dirt years later

They went away to war
and returned crippled in the mind
with the knowledge of all that sticky death
the feel of the trigger gently squeezed
the memory of love cheaply bought
and the soft curve of the rifle stock
against the cheek

And who's to come back whole
to such a country where childhood's fled?
taken to its heels
turned tail
fled down the long hard hill
to nowhere in particular
here where we live

The secret of it all the sound
the haunting sound
always the movement of air
the wail of death
climbing the bitter stairs of history

who's crying in the kitchen?
who's sobbing below the stairs?
whose voice of complaining in the tool shed?
in the garden who's the champion of distress
in the hour when the sky is folded in upon us?

when the voice of god
is once again walking in the garden
stopping to pull a weed
or snap a milldewed flower
full of his own wisdom

the proud and sorrowful voice of god
with its own particular lamentation
as in the cycle of creation rank gardens grow
the fig tree ever barren

The secret of it all the indistinct notation
the space
the dusty space between the galaxies
and the pits in the fabric of existence
the dust is alive
with the precious abstract mystery
of the beginning and end
that fills us all
that fills the perfect cup of nothingness
the room between us and the sun
between the deceitful episodes of our being afloat
in the world of nothing perpetual

The secret of it all
I'll tell you a dream
dreamed repeatedly
the fiercest voice

in the territory of sleep
the anger we notice about us

the secret of it all
we all dream
and our dream is all the same
the same black hand behind us
the songs our children sing echo with it
but dreams are so soon forgotten
the childrens' voices are jangled
with the sound of wheels
and the nervous chatter of the video

yet there's another dream
that even the spaces between the stars
are fecund with the spores of life

but dream telling is an unpopular habit
look at Joseph and his brothers
what they did to him
for constantly assaulting their ears
with his dreaming

The secret of it all
the paradoxical notation
the notion that somewhere in time
there must be justification

our steady progress
over the edge of tomorrow
falling through limitless time
off the edge of our universe
the state of falling
becoming the state of normalcy
being the habit we have of it
the habit of moving always faster
to complete contradiction
to the paradoxical state of coming back
after the great event

having visited the ultimate
and coming back
walking out of the picture house
looking for words to turn into sense
sewn up in a sentence

you've seen it
and expect no more
we've seen it
yet every perception
is a contradiction
to all we believe
as well as every other perception
of the same event

the secret of it all
we've met it and sung about it
but singing leads us into other countries
other ways of observing
the nature of these shared events
the mutating rumours
whispered round our global village

the song moves away
to such a singular territory of the mind
it's hidden from us
behind the fabric of our own ideas

afloat on an ocean
dark with the absence of fishes
clouded to our feel or taste
the smell of decaying vegetation
bubbles of exploding methane
the movement of fire
on the face of the water
Will o' the Wisp
or the Spirit of God.

The secret
you pick it to pieces
with your nervous fingers
truth and fantasy all in shreds
mixed in a small heap

the secret of it all
your careful breath as you wait
as though truth might fall for us
but whoever fell for us?
they smelled our fear
and turned to the other side of our confusion

The secret of it all
you owed us an answer
we owe you a supper
the Queen owes us her love

the bird in the tree sings to us
what shall we do with its song?
fold it in a paper napkin
carefully put it in our jacket pocket
not to crush it
pressed against the heart
bring it home
and breathe it into the radio
a message for those ears
telling us what happened
after lunch the other day

but the bird deprived its song
where did it fly?
the sun is low
and the bird circles the holly tree
hoping to find its song
impaled on the prickles
or caught in the branches like a kite

And so the secret of it all
we run together to the terrific bonfire
that stands for something
at the edges of the retina
it flings up sparks among the dark trees
the poor guy at the apex
stuffed full of fire-works
explodes to the cheers of children

And the secret of it all
I met a man carrying his pack
beside the highway south
was he Christ or Christian?
or that man Jesus off to meet the empire?
Where was he going?
I did not notice movement
only an extended thumb
pointing towards heaven

The secret of it all
Who dug a hole in the rich loam
and whispered his shame
to the ever silent earth?
only the grass heard
and told the cicada
who sang it to the birds
and they
what did they do?
but give it to the rattlesnake
for the life of their fledglings
and the rattlesnake told you
swearing your confidentiality
"....it will go no further for I will bite you"
the secret was petty
but the whisperer was a king
and sometime friend to a minor god

And the secret of it all
deep in the brooding earth
where the serpent sleeps
in the deep silence
only the groaning of the continents
that rub each other in their slow close lying
pressing the rocks to burning liquids
white hot in the darkness of their unimaginable lust

the secret down there you would suppose as safe
but the truth is that secrets
by their nature await telling
like cups await breaking
or mortals death

and as seeds left in the pharoahs tomb
long for a drop of water
to be brought to them across the millennia
to send out two green shoots towards the light
maybe the soul of the king in a grain of rye
or in the sacred smoke from burning hemp?

The secret of it all
the round stone contains
a fossil of a butterfly
full of its colours
a resplendent thing
hidden in a stream washed pebble,
but then in that perfect roundness
maybe it's not there
we can believe
but if we take a hammer and shatter
we destroy the inner in the outer
and are left like an Etruscan tomb
with a specimen fading in air

The secret of it all
we cannot approach or give words
to the sort of thing we can never grasp

the secret of it all
the existence in this small part of space
of a multiplicity of life
we fear might be unique

how can it be?
yet in our panic we look over our shoulder
to discover emptiness
and wonder at the chance accidents
that set us here on this green planet

You wonder at my preoccupation
with the abstracts of biology and space
you wonder at my negligence
this earth of flies
insistent statistics
and news reports

you wonder how in this reality
I turn my telescope away to the stars
that give us age old light through the cold air
so many years acoming
who knows if shining still?

the stars are there that every child wishes on
and now while our humanity
is so severely tested
we turn our eyes up there
hoping for a rescue expedition
that seems so long delaying

so here we are suspended
between heaven and the hard ground
the hungry child

The secret of it all as I am out of touch
but know momentary truths exist somehow
only doubt their form
more interested in the slightly doggy things
that compose my own life

believing maybe that words only cloak
the nakedness of reality
a metaphysical and very decorative
rococco stucco

and maybe Jehovah hit the nail on its head
when he gave his name
like that spinach eating sailor
"I yam what I yam"
and forbade the repetition
of such a simple seeming mystery
and even there is superfluidity
beyond the single affirmation
of an I
or its plurality Is
the self and the self viewing consciousness.

But to travel from the simplicity of the big bang
to the intricate and decadent sophistication
of our luscious biosphere,

from pure purpose
the first plunging waterfall
of energy of existence
to the muddy tideridden delta of entropy
our biological pleasure garden,

from the simplicity that can bear no words
to the playful chaotic mystery
where we find our companions in existence
and grope for something like a map

The secret: there's nothing hidden
the earth stands revealed
as it always has
and in our search for knowledge
what do we hope to find?
a message on a bathroom wall
to say it isn't true?

all that we've seen
and all those rumours
gifts from strangers in elevators
or skid row bars
the last word of a drunk
before he slips into a coma
the muttering of cut lips
and a two day growth of beard

the secret, the search is on
who let it out?
we fear the worst is true
and all else camouflage
the people of this earth
are very beautiful
and very sad
in the light of incipient history

Don't tell me
I don't want to hear.

The secret is:
there is no secret
the dark truth is out
and walking in this world
the feel of the engulfing sea
the return of the homeless word into the mouth
the return of the image to the eye
the retreat of music back into the trumpet
and the trombone spewing from my brain

the world is total knowledge
no hiding place for lies
the lies you tell
are just as vital
as the truth you hide

The secret's out
the words are away from home
the land of Logres
is a free fire zone
and history will turn and savage you
like a mad dog on a suburban street

Dame History has taken off her mask
she wears your face beneath it
your beautiful cosmetic face
with your bitter teeth

but you have an incestuous relationship
with the earth
you fling your shadow
on the field of broken brick
you fling your voice
into the forest of shattered trees
and the field of mud
where the horses died

and between the cities
where the concrete spread
the flikker of video
lights up the skulls of children
and the weeping radio
has caught us in its flood

the enormous secret is flashed on the sky
projected in colour on the low hung clouds
the arrival of the new
is hailed with much excitement
a new dance a new cut of clothes
the poet goes out stands in the coloured rain
sings a song to the rhythm of all he knows

—1984

The Land of Logres is the sacred and mythical Land of the Grail.

The Myth of Adam and Eve

(*an opera in three voices*
God, Narrator, The Children of A&E)
for Gaia and her children, and for Rusty North

Now God planted
a garden in Eden
for Adam and Eve
and he said:

"This garden
I have planted for you
I have filled it
with a million kinds of plants
which will fill your every need;
which will be food for you
and medicine
and the sacred way
of ecstasy.

"Learn of the plants
name them,
find their uses
and nurture my garden
and spare the good things I have made
and the creatures of my fancy.

"Only, I say,
don't eat of the tree,
that one over there
with the lovely flowers
that I put in the centre
of my garden.

"It is the Tree of Knowledge
and has sweet and bitter fruit."

But as you have been told,
the Snake,
or some such manifestation,
persuaded them
to taste the fruit
already tempted, as they were,
by God's own prohibition.

And as Adam and Eve fell
from innocence into knowledge,
so God also fell
into Wrath
and threw Adam and Eve
out of the Garden.

And the Children of Adam and Eve
were very angry at God
and said:

"We will destroy this garden,
We will cut down his trees
and lay waste
the millions of strange plants
he took it into his fancy to grow.

"We will drive out his creatures
so our creatures
which we have bred
with our cunning,
our pigs and sheep and cattle,
can eat grass
and grow fat.

"God gave us the title deed
to this garden.
We will bulldoze it flat
and build ourselves a Mall
and open a car dealership,
a movie theatre
and then a string

of fast food hamburger joints,
"We will call it
'Garden Park'.

"And the parking lots
will be magnificent,
the anchor stores
will be full of soft music,
and the security guards
will rid the neighborhood
of those with no money to spend,
and of the children
with their spray cans,
who sit all day,
play strange music
and dream."

Then God
looked down from Heaven
and said:

"Stupid people!
If you're going to steal fruit,
at least take enough to make a pie.
The Apple you bit
was not yet ripe.

"You're very clever
but you never tasted
the fruit of wisdom
which grew up there at the top of the tree
far beyond your reach.

"Well it's too late now.
That tree went to the pulp mill
long ago.
You made it into
toilet paper.

"I have repented of my wrath.
I have patience.
I'll just sit and watch,
but you won't find me
dodging cars on the freeway."

You'll be wondering
what happened to the fruit of the tree
the sweet fruit
from the topmost branches.

It lay among the slash and fermented
and the ants and wasps
and bears came and ate it
and a few long-haired
tree hugging environmentalists
and a passing logger too.

They all got drunk
on the sweet wine of wisdom
and slept a long season.

And when they awoke
from their strange dreams of knowingness
they decided to bide their time
far away
from the wrathful children
of Adam and Eve
in the deep cities
where clearcuts
will never come.

—1994

Butterflies

You c'd
 and then
  it's a long way back too
but the definitive exercise
 is a laughter
  at the object of desire
   as it,
    he, she
     flees

Oh desire
 I feel it clasp its warm fingers
  in my lymph nodes
you see the rain
 has washed the sidewalk
  of the debris
   of human understatement
and knowledge flutters out
 its knowing gasp upon us

the butterflies are very much aware
 of what they're doing
but we misplace the moment
 as desire crumbles
  and we drift
  and we know less
   each day

It's like summer wind then
 I'm here again
  yes sitting
and the spaces we chose
 for wandering
  are all fouled up
you see

at least the butterflies
 have managed to retain
an objective view of things
 of the critical mass
  of piles of letters
left in a hurry
 by refugees
  from this soft prison

and the riotous indignation
 of butterflies
picketing the blackened sites
 where metaphore has yielded to bulldozed
and the grass has begun
 its assault on the clockface
  of rubble
the ghost of meanderings
 and the abject terror
  of concrete

the butterflies
 once slept by here
left their footprints
 deep in the pages of history
they at least were aware
 and don't doubt it
  afraid

but then, I ask you
 here among the weeds
  the curious growing things
   that are taking over this world
    with vine and seed pod
     and hairy stem
here, I say, don't we all live
 mostly by fear?
by fear and dampness
 and the eternal promise
  of decay?

I won't name no names
 but then among the cabbages
  such things happen
the slugs have waylaid
 an earthworm
  devour it, almost warm
the beans and convolvulus
 make pacts
  to protect each others'
   special spheres of aggression
some stones have lain too long
 and who's to ask
  what's growing in the dark

and from the topmost spires
 of flowering lettuce
the caterpillar leaps —
 awakes
  in falling to a pebbly ruin
a butterfly
 to flap closer to the sun

and from the pulpy fat green flesh
 mouth, guts and rudimentary legs
  a God awakes Icarus like
to soar above the humid mass
 of weeds and soggy mulch
  where far below
   an orange centipede
travels through mouldering stems
 of grass straw
and two black shielded beetles
 carry dung across a clover leaf
a lady bug is out hunting aphids
 and ants ride posse
  to protect their herd
meanwhile the butterflies
 make their lazy way
  through paradise

and the ill matched shape
 of laughter
  quite hungrily watches
   the sleeping cabbage
the disease of darkness
 is about to jump for the moon
 and hold her rind in its teeth
  water squirms in the roots
   the garden crouches in fear
and the groaning caterpillar
 sings a slow song
  to the tooth waiting leaf

and I tell you
 the moon knows its place
  in the night
and I can tell you too
 the caterpillar
  is very fond of the leaf
   it's sitting on
and very soon will eat

 and the slug too — the slug
compostulating time and sunlight
 caught in the form
  of a half eaten strawberry
about to return to the Earth again
 after a sojourn
  as a closer thing to Heaven

and the garden troubled
 with unreasoned laughter
  and you tell me
   it's a sick time to dance
and who am I among the dandelions
 the soft seed that lies
  like spring snow
   soft and wet
among the sprouting grass blades?

the butterflies know all sorts of things
 and most of them deviously
and as for a catalog
 of knowledge gained
  of uncertain journeys
   among proud vegetables
a legend of roots taken
 and strange encounters
by rotten fences
 I could relate it all
  as I have heard it
but butterflies
 to say the word again
  have a devious way of telling tales
and are apt to elaborate
 for theirs is the kinship
  of nonsense -

and in the separate style
 of dancing
  we touch so gently
   the mannerisms of God
the folding of sleep
 comes ultimately to mean
  something for us
beyond the scope
 of touch and smell

but it's all touch and smell
 and the moon sits
  in the sky above us
cocking its horns
 in our direction
sending howls of derision
 across the night

beyond the end of the street
 is the water
and beyond the water
 mountains, rock

and pinetrees
pockets of decaying snow
  where the sun never reaches
  and ridges and mountains
    stretching beyond imagination
and here a garden
  where butterflies dance
  a small outpost of wilderness
in a tapestry of stone

Oh, butterflies, butterflies
  you learn to dream
even in dreaming there is method
  among the stones
    camomile
among the hot stones
and butterflies dance
  above the horizon
flat stretched land
  of great distance
  in every direction
here North, here East
  West and South
these peculiar directions
  one way the snow will come from
one way birds will fly
  the sun rising
  ways of travellers
    and rivers

I'm telling you something
  you know quite well
but we should make nests
  in our mind, for old knowledge
  and pamper it (with tea maybe
    and cookies)
  before we can hope to show hospitality
to any new marvels

the Dragon awakes in the East
 the Ogopogo and Sasquatch
  roar out defiance
the sleepy old volcanoes
 of the western hills
  yawn and stretch
have you ever seen a volcano
 clean its teeth?
the wonderful things
 that rear at the four points
  the Northern Lights
   running this way and that
but I'm writing of one land
 and sitting in another
where the fog blows in off the sea
 and the gulls are not above
  pecking garbage

and the sea is so greenly proud
 though almost loath
  to neighbour us
   uneasy pimples
    on the planets surface
  lacking comprehension
   of a size
    beasts never sought
restless running soars
 of hunger
  and misplaced dream

and the gulls know
 the value of garbage
  on a scale
   we can't compute
the delicacy
 the riches we reject
  but that's the stoney surface
   of our guilt
while we wander
 from image to image

from hunger to hunger
the moment slipping
 always ahead of us
  into the future
   as we're left here
    standing dumbfounded

So we believe
 and even our belief
  we hedge
   with so many conditions
that belief
 even belief
  fails to give liberation

You ask me to leave off talking
 and conjure images
  turn abstractions to pictures
   illuminate
the gull by the garbage can
 the lid lying on the ground
  What do you want?
   Better Poetry?
Voicier? More picturesque?

When I say "Animals"
 you want them to jump
  off the page
so you can shoot them down
 with your immaculate
  machine guns
You ask me for butterflies again
 but the first frosts have come
  they've laid their eggs and died
and the fat caterpillars
  are sleeping
   somewhere
   you probably won't find

—1973

Poems From The Heart

AND POEMS FROM THE HEART
 and the bowels and the spleen
  poems from the kidneys
   and the urinary tract
poems from the different lobes
 of the brain
  from the right brain
   the left brain
    the mid brain
     the back brain

 poems from the base of the spine
poems from the souls of the feet
 poems from the bits that I have
  and you don't
poems from the bits that you have
 and I don't (those are your poems)

  poems from hair
   and fingernails
    from armpits
     and toenails

poems, as I say from the heart
 all those poems
  crawling like maggots
from every part of the corporate structure
 structured poems
  anatomicly correct poems
   politicly correct poems
poems for the year 1993 (or 4, or 5)
 politicly correct poems
  for the political mess we're in

poems full of answers
 but no questions

poems also with lots of questions
 like "Wot's the way to the Jon?"
"Where can I find a cheap hotel?"
  "Do you like cheese?"
"Sorry, I don't speak your language
 could you show me the phrase
    in the phrase book?"
"Even the street sellers speak their funny English
 and it's good fun to beat their prices down"

 But as I was saying
  before I went off on holiday —
Poems from the heart
 the left ventrical
  the right aurical
the superior vena cava
 and all the other parts
  I forgot the names of

So I say
 poems in the blood
  like spirochetes
   or corpuscles
   or viruses
like malignant tumors
 in the blood
Poems come around for us
 with each beat of the heart

hungry poems
 hanging out at the mall
post historical post literate poems
 watching buttocks
  on the corners of the street
watching cop comedies
 laughter and death on the video

anatomicly correct poems
 with cocks and balls and cunts
  and breasts
   and armpit hair and real blood

Poems by fax from E. Jerusalem
 poems by fax from Jo'burg
  from Sarajaevo
   from E.LA

Suspect poems with versions of history
 politicly incorrect locked up and hidden
  nice poems and nasty poems
Sad proud poems from proud sad people
 some of us might like to forget
poems scrawled on bathroom walls
 by victims of political necessity
  with shaved heads
   and shiny chains
thoroughly nasty poems
 I wouldn't ask you to read
nasty poems in nasty language

Nasty poems
 poems from the heart
not my heart
 mine like yours beats pure
  as riven snow
poems from hearts but
 like city snow in march
  black and piss yellow
east of the mountains back in the old days
 before our automobilic climactic changes

Poems from the heart
 from the spray can
from the magic marker like children died for
 fierce poems beaten from the drum
  with teeth filed painfully
   to sharpened points

Street heart poems
 from unemployment lines
  from welfare lines
from the beauty parade at the local cop shop
 from prison lines
  lines of poems
   from the heart
   blood lines
poems from the heart

And as I say
 Poems from the heart
and the guts, and the spleen
 from fingernails
  and toenails
 and the hairs that grow along your arm
and poems from the eye
 that contracts and expands
  as it searches my face
and the song of your breath
 and the movement of hair
  with the turn of a head

and poems
  from the centre of love
from the dark flowering places
 of bodies
  flowing with love
and poems
 from fingers
  in the celebration
   of love
of nerves
 which unite themselves
  body to body
   in the orb, the empire of love
the dark turning world
 the one unity of love

Poems from the heart
 and the breath and the tongue
  from bellies and thighs
   navel crotch and anus
from the dark wooded country
 and the magnificent pillar of sex
  from the breath of eyes
and the landscape of muscle and bone

Poems from the heart
 from the laughter that rules the heart
from the song of our being one
 even across the miles
  even down the hiway
   through alien cities
    of overpass, on ramps
     bus terminals
    and all night eateries
poems down the long landscape
 the telephone wire
  the heart that connects us
the whole quivering, beating heart of night
 moment in moment

poems from the heart
 your poem and my poem
  a perfect stumbling dance
between hither and yonder
 down the long hiway
  through veins and nerve cells
the touch of your heart
 beating in my heart
poems from the heart
 from the bright twittering
  bird filled morning of hearts

Poems from all the hearts
 of the round earth
  beating their tune of love
affirming the way of life

59

the ritual of the heart
that is sacred to all of us
 that binds us
each in a secret private exstacy
 the enfolding exstacy
  of all things on the earth
all the pulsing trembling weaving
 laughing
  traceries of life stuff
the plasmic consciousness
 of the fruitful dancing earth
this heart bound orb
 in the fecund ocean of space
where the song of life
 is the great song
  the unified theme
   of the choir of love
the unified field theory
 of the science of love
the movement of life
 always to a further exstacy
  the dark dreaming
   of the turning of love

Poems from the mother
 the heart of Gaia

 —1991

Notes:
I began this poem as a sentimental love poem, to a woman who was
threatened with medical heart procedure. The poem soon took on a life of
its own, demanding a much deeper and more ironic approach than I was
about to give it.

    The questions are taken from various phrase books, except the
first which is taken from 'The Zoo Story' by Edward Albee, and the snide
comments about bargaining down prices, often heard from the mouths of
habitual tourists. The Children who died for the magic marker, were exe-
cuted in the latter days of the Iranian revolution, the older found guilty of
political graffiti, and the younger for crying.

Because of the white paper,
because of a word upon it
a word not discovered yet
not revealed yet
because of the hoodlum shape of the word
casting its shaddow behind the paper
slightly to the right of the ear that is listening
so intently
    at the keyhole of the paper
because of the distance
of the ear from the eye
    making its tracks
    across the shimmering paper
because of the air
    about the word
    that hides itself
        behind the paper
and wells into utter vacuum
    in the garden of chaos
    beyond the paper
because of the ear that hears
and forgets to inform the brain
because of the time
of the meaning of the word
that is lost in history
    hidden in dictionaries
and buried under stones
    beside broken factories
    and turbines forever
        spilling their water
and buried under sod
    by the bones of horses
    on inglorious battlefields
        in unnamed pastures
where the sound of the word
    is breathed by gasses
        of decomposition
        of the debris of ages
because of the silence
    and the whiteness of the paper
    I cover it with words
        and avoid saying anything

Pleasures of Existence
for Ed Varney

AS YOU SAY
WE MUST GET THROUGH ALL
THIS   ALL OUR DOUBTS
YOU SAY: "IN A DARK WOOD
—

Pathological Warmongering

Oh Gardener
as you lay your mulch
upon the earth
the rustling dead leaves
left from spring
which were green once
where dandelions sleep
waiting for the wheel
to move another
quarter turn
a quadrant
a historic moment
fling all life
into another
evolving year

IN A PARKING LOT FILLED
WITH SUNSHINE, NO SHADY
PLACE ONLY DANDELIONS
WHICH WILL, YOU KNOW
FINALLY TAKE OVER EVERYTHING
OUR CITY REPRESENTS OR IS
IN THE MIDDLE OF LIFE

the image of the world
our conceptual equivalence
a dream of fire
green islands

under ice
the tides that turn and turn
and burnish us
so round
and history
like wind blown sand
that fills our crevices
and the small flowers
of ongoing existence
bloom above
long deep water-searching roots
not established in experience
but born upon it
maybe

HALFWAY ALONG OUR WAY
STRAYING IN A PARKING LOT
BESIDE A CONCRETE WALL
STALL SPACES MARKED, DIVIDED
WITH YELLOW PAINT
BETWEEN THE DOG AND THE CROW
AND THE CLOCK THAT TELLS US
THAT TIME IS NO OBJECT
I MET ONE, AS ONE DOES
ALIGHTING FROM A PARKED CAR

A CHEVY UNDOUBTABLY IT WAS

You guessed it right
we carried home
to our significance
the final name
of God
the parameters
of that internal space
where the seed hides itself
unripening
waiting for a voice
full of such things
as terrify us

but here we wait indeed
the secret things
among the everlasting flowers
in the garden of our disbelief

WHO DEMONSTRATED IN A MANNER
OF SPEAKING THE TECHNIQUE OF
DESCENDING, INDICATING THE WAY
TO BARGAIN BASEMENTS, MEN'S
WASHROOMS AND HOT DOG STANDS
IN UNDERGROUND MALLS
HE DESCRIBED THE WAY THE BUSSES
RUN ABOUT AND HOW THE NURSES
ATTEND THE WOUNDED IN THE
BURN WARD AT THE HOSPITAL
IN THE PARKING LOT THIS

Indeed
at the untidy edge
of the epitomy
of our desire
we stand here glued
to the absense
of our memory

the ideal of our
maliferous designs
quite occasionally
rooted us in longing

the abscess of our
unhappy faithfulness
we are aground
you do believe it too

as though
the world were flat again
and all those ships
were sailing off the edge
into perfect nothingness

the soul of God
OBVIOUS METAPHORE FOR HUMAN
EXISTENCE, AMONG VEHICLES NEW
AND OLD, BATTERED AND WELL
CARED FOR. WE SAT DOWN ON A
LOW CONCRETE DIVIDER AND
SHARING A DEEP BREATH OF SMOKE
HE LED ME URGENTLY AND TENDERLY

Where is the power in the land?

the man who calls the shots
that man person
the mad man person
in the deep concrete
bunker

tomorrow is his birthday

la terra trembla
and the earth shakes
'momy, dady, why is the earth shaking?'

gone to sea
gone to the hills
gone to ground
close to the scene
of our undoing
the dead cars
rusting in the street

human sympathy
diluted
in bad water

destabilised
the orbit
of this world

AMONG THE RIDDLES OF EXISTENCE
THE ANCIENT KNOCK-KNOCK JOKES
I CAN NEVER REMEMBER —
IN THIS PARKING LOT
I'VE TOLD YOU ABOUT THE PARKING

hidden you see
these depths
you arrive at the site
of our amazing

the foolish land
pilloried in history
the fact of our partition
the memory of the sea
the breath of your
magnificence

in idleness I write
my life spread out
over there
the dereliction of duty

you warned me
and as I'm here
on the otherside
of nowhere special
writing all landscape
into a comma
all experience
into a pause for breath

this elegant emptiness
the reflection in my eye
we inhabit a small portion
of our conception
and the rest is carrion fields
for pecking crows
and so ideally we arrive

LOT, WITH ITS CONCRETE WALLS
ITS DANDELIONS, ITS YELLOW LINES
AND FINALLY THE LOW CONCRETE

Our own words
barely our own
you dig deep
tunneling
in the uncertain shale
roof props
and fire damp
at home
inside the hill
cohabiting
with death
and injury
tunneling the skull

and the man
with that enormous voice

"here! here! here!"
you call
the fog is heavy
upon the earth
the signals out on the water
the voice of this town

the seagulls
and the semis
drag-arsing up Nicol hill

and in my thoughts
sailing away
to Africa

DIVIDER WHERE WE SHARED
A SACRAMENT OF SMOKE AND
HE DETAILED TO ME
THE MAGNIFICENT PARADOX OF

a few words
a few words on my plate
the cat walks over
carefully
to drink from
the jug of milk

my language
becoming minescule
my experience
closed in
unimportant

I cannot write a poem
to impress you with my wisdom
I'm unimpressed myself
I can only write a poem
to display
the few words
on my plate
show how they articulate
like chicken bones
and how the cat
is stalking a fly
that feeds luxuriously
in the spilled garbage bag

THE INEXCUSABLE AND ETERNAL
VIOLENCE THAT IS THE
EXISTENCE OF GOD AND THE
MOMENTARY PASSAGE OF LOVE
IN THE PARKING LOT WHICH
AMONG THE CLOUDS OF SMOKE

the eternal confrontation
at the edges of the retina
still here
where memory flickers
we're still here

bliss and hunger
certainty
where there is none

an elected god
in the garden of flies?

God the majesty
of all creation
the turner
of fortune's wheel
mankind plummets down

our pride in holding fast
the primacy of man
the universe
will sing on
or grind on
even as the dust
settles among the relics
of the human race

AND EXHAUST FUMES SEEMED
INDISTINGUISHABLE FROM THE
WHOLE HISTORY OF MANKYNDE
AND THE CLEVER BEASTS HE
THINKS HE'S DESCENDED FROM
IN THIS PARKING LOT THE MAN

words make themselves
in this silence
an array
of arguements
in which we find
no fingerhold
no certainty
our expectations
in unsatisfaction
in this winterland
this acre of frost

ultimate territory
of frozen toes

absolution
we could always travel
back in history
to the edge of out world
to the point of incision
the intersection
of the frame of reality
with that field of daisies
where we lay
that day

the sweet events
of a momentous story
the divination
of the unconscious mind

FROM THE CHEVY ENLIGHTENED
ME AND LED ME THROUGH THE DEPTHS
WHERE IT IS NECESSARY TO CRAWL TO
POKE AND PROBE AT THE ROOTS OF

Over ripe
the places we've been at
so difficult to describe
so completely undistinguished
anonymous
distinctive
only by a slight smell
that lingers
of burning leaves, maybe
of spawning fishes
maybe an area
merging at the edges
to stretches
where the air is tainted slightly
with melted plastic
or hot motor oil

but somewhere
in this odiferous
geography
in the broken grass
we have a small spot
held sacred
by some thin familiarity
maybe

LIFE AND THE MEANINGS WE
MIGHT ATTACH IF WE EXAMINED
IT ALL WITH ENOUGH ATTENTION
TO RANK GRASS AND DUSTY SHRUBS
FLOWERING DIRTILY IN THE
BREATH OF AUTOMOBILES AND OLD

I've seen the place
we met ourselves in once
and came away
disjointed
amazed
by the birth
of our mythology

and since then
the manner
of our creation
and how we slid
to such a present state

we passed the tree
where God is said to hide
and small animals twitter
in its fire blasted womb

NEWSPAPER DECAYING UNDER THE
WEIGHT OF UNCARED FOR NEWS
AND THE STOCKMARKET PRICES
LIKE SO MANY NAILS HAMMERED
INTO THE CRUCIFIED FEET OF THE

DYING GOD OF CENTIPEDES
AND THE FLASH OF REFLEXION
FROM BROKEN POP BOTTLES, NO
LONGER WORTH A DIME IN
DANGEROUS FRAGMENTATION
AMONG THE CIGARET BUTTS IN A

Unable to awaken
and in our time
such a heap
of dreaming
oh the round earth
contains us
in its roundness
it's home
you see
unable as individuals
to reach escape velocity
we're here for good
or till we rot away

also
seasonally – in our totality
beneath us
hiding
the fat slug
it has knowledge
a gift for all these
skeptical philosophers

Go to the slug
observe its ways
and be wise

NEGLECTED CORNER AND SOW
THISTLES WITH THEIR CORONETS
OF SEED FLUFF LETTING FLY
AT HEAVEN ON THE CURLING WIND
THAT EXPLORES THE PARKED CARS
AND THE TOURISTS OF THE HUMAN

the land in darkness
where the creatures move
Who will tell you
what they've seen?

the object of terror
that accompanies you
clutched at your back
just beyond your sight

return to the edge
look into the sea of illusion
to see your maker's face
the eyes you avoided

even in your dream
a bad time
such a taste
in your mouth

CONDITION WHO SIT ON A CONCRETE
DIVIDER PASSING A SORT OF
CIGARET BACKWARDS AND FORWARDS
WITH THE CONVERSATION IN A
PARKING LOT BY A CONCRETE
WALL AMONG THE CHEVYS FORDS
AND HONDAS WHERE THE DANDELIONS
BLOOM AND THE BLOWN NEWSPAPER

Oh,
You know the way we are
we were
and might have been
and what we will become
you're familiar
with our habit
the way we stand
and turn
and greet the day
daily

after such a night
we might have had
you know our habits
and how we manage them
you are quite sure
of our enjoyments
of existence
as we enjoy it daily
and venture nightly
into some eternity
and swim upon
some oceans of our being
our sleepwalking
our travelling
hilarious fulfillment
and you understand
the very abstract notion
of my being here
in this orange coloured
coffee shop writing

ASCENDS HEAVENWARDS BUT FALLS
BACK EXHAUSTED AND EVERYTHING
FAILING TO AVOID BEING A

O know that voice
the insolent
in isolation
insolvent
insoluable
dissolved
as it might seem
in a river which flows
from the mawkish cave
of historical nonsense
out and about and about
We've been passengers
carried to that gravel bank
on the edge
of a naked continent

METAPHOR FOR THE STATE
OF MAN IN THIS RIDICULOUS

Once
albeit the time
of wandering
up and down
peering into stores

the view of ourselves
our fierce activity
caught in the window glass

the street for us
our walking
in an inevitable
flood of faces
and attitudes
streaming towards us
like history herself

The quality of a dream
all the parables
of the apocalypse
parabolas
and what word shall I use
far away, hypotanuse
here we suffer
here as the world might choose
what love can I abuse?
at teatime listening to the news

Self doubt self doubt
drives us to art
drives us apart
and back through art
to the hot and sticky abyss
of the heart

EXISTENCE OF THE NOBLE
SAVAGE WHO HAS LOST HIS
NOBILITY WITH THE ADVENT
OF PARKING LOTS AND DAY-OLD
NEWSPAPERS
WHICH NEVER QUITE MAKE IT

at the edge
crossing the line
divided by a margin
of error

untold destruction
obviously
waiting
all these words
pile up
ineffectual at the slaughter

you wait
you listen
do you hear the birds

do you hear
another litter of baby rats
in the basement?

CLIMBING UP THE WIND
IN THE DUBIOUS ASCENT

they are all here
all the people
and each one of them
filled with a certain
and uncertain vision
their eyes
capable of fire
their darkness
fecundity

we saw them
the people
in arrival
with their burdens
their baggage
and belongings
waiting
standing upon the earth

the people have come
they hold their heads
towards the stars
their feet towards
the hot deep iron core

TO THE MAD HEAVEN
OF NEWSMEN

Once we were
and you signal us
across the water
the fire, the fight
the terror in your eyes
silence has struck you
across the lips
your black flag beckons us
the sea full of rocks
what haven for us?

We have a garden
we exercise it daily
with seeds and rake.
Among the balling cabbage
and the pumpkins
running everywhere
we believe we find
a small space to root ourselves
but maybe it's illusion
maybe the worm
arrived there first

another child
to be born
eyes to be open
to this startling world
Voyager
like an Irish monk
in a boat of skin
to the happy isles
the isle of sheep
the congealing sea
what blessing can I give you
or any compass bearing?

—1983

Ode for Gaia

What voice for the wind
 the knowledgeable
  the far traveling
   ancient wind
that blew us wherever
 and whenever
into the mouth of the sea
 the canyon streets
  grit in the teeth
Depths of wind
 and great mouths of our joy
the quiet moment in the heart
 of the wind
 when all rage is suddenly stilled
the teeth of the wind
 hungrily chewing at us
the cold north
 and the parched desert wind
  traveling whole continents
weighed down with the dust
 of inexhaustible hiways
 and the poisonous smoke
  of burning plastic

The wind, proud answer
 at the beginning of time
in the whole dark twist
 of your imagination
and the memory of ancient seas
 of beaches washed by tides
  since life itself was slime
   foam flung and sun dried
    in wave licked rock pools

This Earth defined in movement
 vortices of foul weather

79

moving in from the coast
snow on desert mountains
 the rushing of rivers
  their tumbling brown load
   of the good earth
the gnawing of ice on granitic rock
 the treasuries of ancient beaches
and the edging and shoving
 of continents
uprearings and shudderings
 in their unimaginable lust
the slow deep noise of grinding
 and rubbing in the hot core
  What dark dreams!
Pulsations of Magma
 and Iron hot and thick as blood

What dreams this Earth?
this precious ball with its fierce heart?
 here suspended between
  the sea and the rock   between
   fire and ice — this edge
this memory hidden in our humblest cells
 of our first journeying
  in water and sunlight
  and the rocks at the tide edge
   the safe crevices — the algal gardens
where we might live out
 our being and becoming
  our discovery of this realm of life

Seas, rivers, gardens, fires,
   the light
the gestation of the word in fecund silence
 and the memory
  the echo of the word
whispered through the dusty universe
 writing itself in the scratchings
  of historians

the exhalation, the explanation
 of our brutality, of our inadequacy

And the Word lies on history
 like a morning's dew
  on long grass,
awakens
 like the dawn chorus
  the spring singing of joyful birds,
the voice of history
 the aria that moves
  among the mountains
the break of sunlight
 against the glass towers
and in the dusty weedfilled backyards
 of the awakening city
  shabby in the dawning
and in the rising poisoned breath
 of automobiles
  the cry of a child.

And beyond us, in imagination
 is our history
  and the unspoken word —

  Dust Soil Roots
the kingdom of fungae
 and nematodes
the dark passage of ants
 and the slow wise worm
  ingesting as she goes
   the flesh of Earth
    grazing on soil, bone dust
   blood country
warm food for onions and dandelions
 and last years leaves

Say it with flowers
 say it with taproot and runners

fruiting bodies of deep carrion feeders
 Say it with darkness
and the seepages of rich water
 with the mulch of leaves
  and potato peelings
with the world of heat
 the waiting world
waiting for sunheat or rain fall
 seed world, root world
  bacterial faunas
   quietly building Eden

Say it with thistle and bramble
 and hot shit
  say it with flowers
Say it with pollen and pistil and stamen
 with the seed and the sperm
  with moth tongue, the flight of bees
   and the humming bird

And seeds caught by the wind
 born aloft, higher than bird flight
making their voyage
 to the edge of space
where the hot tides of the sun
 flow in fearful currents
in the deep restless moments of space
 on the edge of our living
the fierce cold burning edge
 of our being here
Vortices, Whirlpools of solar winds
 the hot pulse of naked fire

Who can resist
 who can withstand
  the sun's fire
that like a mother bear
 licked us into being
  such a long time ago?   —1993

Dancing the small game tender (a poem for tambourine)
for the Nanaimo Coffee House

Idleness the small game – tender
 let us dance
  the small game
  tender
the snake
 the old snake
  I know that snake
  the small game
  I know the snake
 let us dance
  the old snake
  let us dance
   the small game
let us dance the small game – tender

 let us dance
  the small game
  let us dance
   the naked man
   let us dance
    the old snake
 I know the dance
  the old snake
  let us dance
   the small game
   tender

eyes
 eyes in the grass
  the wind is full of eyes
  let us dance
   wind in the eyes
 let us dance
  voices in the wind
  let us dance

voices in the grass
let us dance
calling up the snake
let us dance
eyes in the dust
voices in the dust

let us dance
voices for the snake
let us dance the small game
tender
let us dance
sweat in the eye
let us dance the small game
tender
let us dance — a cloud of sweat
let us dance — the small game
glistening sweat — the small game

voices in the dance
eyes in the dust
tears in the dance
let us dance
the small game
tender

let us dance
give me your feet
let us dance
swing your bellies
let us dance
thighs and breasts
arms and sweat in the eye
let us dance the small game
tender

Let us dance
I'll see you among the stars
let us dance

I'll meet you in the bright water
let us dance
 it's snow and it's dust
  let us dance
   the small game
    tender

Let us dance
 "is not the city a place of song?"

let us dance
 "would you say that the city
  is the abundance of life?"

let us dance
 "are not the streets
  a dancing throne?"

let us dance the small game
 tender

Let us dance
 as the smokey wind moves round this
  lovely ball called Earth

let us dance
 as the fishy, oil dark sea
  washes this home
   where we dance and laugh and cry

let us dance
 as the good earth
  that is under our fingernails
   is the giver of life

let us dance — the good Earth
 let us dance
  our one true love
   Earth

let us dance
 the mother
  bearing down
   and hurling us bodily
    into this world

let us dance
 the father
  bearing up
   and conjugating our tenses
    in all the dark tunnels
     of their tender night

let us dance
 our ancestors
  the monkeys and lemurs
   the little hairy creatures
    and the fish that climbed
     on a mud bank
and their ancestors also
 the unsophisticated lumps
  of vital cells
our unrecognizable laughing ancestors
 let us dance
  the small game
   tender

 Let us dance
the Father   the Mother
the Sun and the Moon
 let us dance
  the Galaxy
   let us dance
    the small game

Let us dance
 small music in laughter
  the sunlight
   and the night

86

let us dance
 your hand
  and your eye
let us dance
 your voice on the edge of it
  you move with a swagger
let us dance — tender
 the small game
  tender

Death comes for the dying man
 let us dance
  for death the small game
the dying woman
 dances with Death
we've met them both
 doing the double dance
  tender and wild the dance of death
tender her small game
 leaping the widdershins of her dance
the contrary laughing dance of death
 and we dance
  for the woman in death
   tender our feet
    in the dust
tender our laughter
 tender the song of our dance
  dancing for death
   the small game
    tender

dance for the dying man
 easing the anger of death
  dancing for laughter and pity
the shining of death
 dance for the soft womb taking
  the small game tender of death

Dance for the sunlight
dance for bright water
the green leaves
and the smokey eye
dance for the small game
the small game of all of it
dance for the small game
the small game tender.

—1981

Ol' Ma River
(for the river we call the Fraser and all her sisters)

Here we are
this land of our silence — gone
Oh country
  of the treasure of dust

fish river spawn river
 sturgeon river
  salmon river
duck river
 goose river
  eel river
river of small voices
 of songbird and cricket
frog river
 in the marshes
marsh river
 oh sweet wilderness
oh sweet tongue
 flood of snowmelt
  sweet silences
   bitter silences
river on the damp edge
 of the city
where do you flow to?
 where do you flow from?
what dreams
 from the mountains to the sea?
  Oh sweet river
   oh sweet wilderness

Who are you?
 what names do you come with?
what several names
 from the mountains
  the snow cap

the glacier
you flow through many languages
 what bridges rapids rocks
  still pools
slow lazy stretches of river
 where under hanging trees
  insects skate
 on the surface of the water
gravel banks, nurseries
 for salmon small fry
What do you flow through
 what languages?
  what ancient names?
what peoples gathering
 by river bank
  and fishruns?
 oh sweet wilderness
what rapids and whirlpools
 what industries, paintshops
plating shops, pulpmills
 feed lots, pig farms
power lines, storm drains
 what oily mess
  running off the hiway
what landscapes of obscenity
 what desolation, what desecration
  what do you flow through
  in what languages
with what strange molecules
 chlorinated poly-phenols and
exotic benzene derivatives
 and many others
that I don't know the names of
 How sad your journeying
  in what languages
 what languages of fish
  the white belly of poisoned fish
what languages you flow through
 of effluent

90

of outfall
 of depletion
  of starvation
of oxygen depletion
 of oxygen starvation
of heavy metals
 of battery shops
  of plating shops
of farmers' fields
 of fertilizer
  of pesticide
What languages you flow through?
 How can my tongue respond?
How can my tongue but feel
 the bitter metallic edge
  of those languages?
How we define the sacred in desecration?
How we scarred the sacred?
How we took water
 from the sacred
drove it through the turning wheels
the turbines of our money machine
 sold it down the river!
How we scarred the sacred
 sold it down the river!
What languages you flow through
 what fickle tongues
  what languages you flow through
   in policy, in politics!
 scarred the sacred
what languages you flow through
 oh sweet river
  oh sweet wilderness.

 Have you deserted us?
waiting till we sleep the long sleep
 will you then return?
 Oh sweet wilderness
what barren wildness in the hearts

of men, of women
 oh sweet wilderness
 oh sweet wilderness
What languages you flow through
 what histories
  what grammars
   what grimmoires
 what futures imperative!
what words you lay upon the tongue
 Oh river
  oh sweet wilderness

Waiting silent garden
 patient (to some degree)
  infinitely patient
measuring the seasons of man
 between freeze up and run off
carved the canyon
 through long sleepy eons
  waiting again
   in the drifting continents
for us to become
 another memory in stone
  between our fate
  and our history
damage repaired
 waiting for the ice to come again
and scrape the old earth clean
 of all our infamy
  this upstart species
finding its way to dust
 down the slow rivers
and how shall I say it?
 oh memory
  oh sweet wilderness.

 —1993

Like Stepping Stones above the Traffic
(for Briar Kari taken by Cancer, July 1987)

Dreams and Odors

Tod
Muerte
Our language has become
unaccustomed
now we see you
now we don't
and then so quietly you escaped us
slipping into the future
leaving us standing here
totally dumbfounded

and here another August's heat
is beating on our heads
and Heaven is not close to us
and every night comes back
with all its dreams and odors

The Vaste Parched Solipsism

How many hours on its debit sheet
life marked us down
a bad risk
in all the kitchens of inspiration
and back sheds
of dubious creativity?

These roots, these threads of sense
we looped and twined
through all our memories
and these reproaches
of our particular infirmities

93

and you then, in that last loneliness
the desert, the Gobi
the vaste parched solipsism
of your suffering

and I, this idle man
the eye within the mirage
and all that stony plain between us
of unshareable experience

The wordy house of ill repair

So we say
'Love' & 'Death'
& 'Suffering'

But look you how these words are threadbare
in the patched cloth of language
the ripped shirt, torn trousers
we call vocabulary

These rampaging feelings hold us captive
in the wordy house of ill repair
as desperately as once we spun
those erstwhile raptures for us
the industry of memory
in the ramshackle house of love

and we are now most
physiologically afraid
sleep fitfully in dusty attics
lie singly in the house of sorrows

Above the traffic

Imagine us as we have reached
where Heaven has hid us
and your words
like stepping stones above the traffic
at this intersection
in no persons' land

and you, how you passed over
went on before, got promoted
bought the farm —

and the radio overflows
down the hallways of this house
where the dead lie sleeping
where Death embarrassed us
and left us without words
as you took departure from us
in this world full of highways

Here we are again
mythic hitchhikers, sans destination
with our naked thumbs out
cooling in the rain

Some new words

And we must fabricate
some new words
as beyond reflection
since that moment
when our dictionaries were pillaged

For the word 'Death' I shall say
'Star'
for the word 'dead' I will write
'green'

for you are green,
the star has taken you
then for 'die' we shall say 'plant'
and for 'mourn' or for 'fail'
use the word 'sow'

You planted, became green
the Star took you
I sowed my seed
in this dry summer

A half full bottle of beer

You left us standing there
on the dock, waving
as you hoisted all your flags
and sailed over the horizon

and we are left
with the tawdry business of living
as once in a railway station
sitting all day as it were
staring at a half full bottle of beer

My heart was filled those days
overburdened with you
like a lump of dough

Age long
and limited
these words
return to their dictionaries

The dark hours of forever

Once again
returning to your memory
to the pain of lost joy
folded in a touch
your hand

These moments
that trap us
a knife within the wound
how you left us!

Become enamored then with Death
beyond the measures
that might presume to poetry

the insubstantial substance of my thought
evaporates
as I could never reach you
will you bless me then
in the dark hours
of forever?

Perfectly at ease

But we are cautious people
in the house of forever
and all these words
I never said to you
What did I try saying?
as only now your absence waits for me

Suddenly we discover geographies
in this world's sorrow

Perfectly at ease
in your old jealousy
and sometimes then we walked home
You in your discovery

The clouded window

You met us that day
You saw us then
through the clouded window
of your mortality

Such words!
and the silence sprouting with words

We touched despair then
You left on the last train
we felt like taking a trip
to a country
where they speak a different
language

Our world is very ordinary
we draw our maps around it
all so easily perceived

For such is the poverty of words
we put all poetry behind us
a disease of clouded images

The saddest animals

It was a loan of dreams
You reflected us in all our vanity
saw the movement
that enjoyed the moment of our faces

despite us all
it was the best that we could manage

All the saddest animals
are hiding from us
You knew
how we stretched into fragments of winter
to all those figments
wherever you imagined us

Unlikely to observe
the dream we counted for
islands of spite

how the accusation of the night
was held against us

The hedgehog and the mole

Time matched us
with all that effort we found wanting
the touch of it
its rub and itch
a small unlikely moment
in this history of standing still

This laughter
the balance and least unlikely trick
Cupid pulled out of an opera hat
and the obliteration of all your sinful cities
with their sticky heat

And the saddest animals
the hedgehog
and the mole
the mayflie
and daddy-long-legs

The woodlouse and the earwig

The slow creatures
the blind
and the shortlived
the grossly misunderstood
the woodlouse and the earwig

It seems we know you
yet you escaped our lust
the welcome gardener
how deceitful this city is
in all its glass

You saw our eyes within it
this moment in the dance
and another way
we've all been speaking
see how we wear our mouths
it seems, with ostentation
like oystershells

Picture postcards of desire

What small games
we've been playing
within the reflection of the year
in marl and clay
the story of crushed rocks

Small circles of hope
small as the sea
and the eelgrass

You build your maps
but the names have all got
washed away somehow
the houses are all

picture postcards of desire
and the traffic of history
is waiting
by deserted traffic lights

The illusion of music

though history, they say
is all the better off for lack of us
like this house
with its account of cockroaches

And now the darkness
calls out our names
silence is on ration
the sound of voices
running like dirty water
the house of winter

the illusions of music
the difficult sounds of your imagination
the sea is all forks
the stairs of the sea
booby trapped with small deadly toys
the disadvantage of the sea
in this last hungry season

The bullfrogs are bellowing

You gnaw at the edge of the tide
at the piled unremarkable bodies
left when the water retreated
jetties of rusty bones
and skulls floating on the water's surface
marking the channel
between quicksand
and mudbank

The polished basalt
of your cranium
holds a black idea
and the bullfrogs are bellowing
in snakeswamp
the crickets sing their song
quite satisfied with darkness

You heard the ravens laughing

and in the salt marsh
dunebound seepages
of cutting grass
and stunted willow trees
in the brackish water
the amorous amorphous complexity of birds
and civilizations of little fish

Pigs rooting for acorns
among the barbed wire
of invasions that threatened our childhood
and then the long hills
landscapes of sleeping women

warriors to awaken
shake their sodden tresses
at some final battle day

You heard the ravens laughing
by other seas
the siren song of sealions and walrus

and the old waves
have set their footprint
within the bonecase
of your desire

The hiss of eggs

How you remember us
mud monday
corned beef, canned
steak and kidney pudding
launched darkly in the house
of your oblivion
The hiss of eggs
the memory of salty bacon

The Spirit of God moved on the waters
and the voice of God went awalking
in the gardens
in the cool of the day
the voice of God
arose from his siesta
and went a strolling by the fountains

The wind is full of jasmine

In the cities of figleaves
and parade grounds of flower gardens
houses of fishtanks
and summer night
when the wind is full of jasmine

103

and you knew us
on the brittle hillside
of perfect glass
and cruel grapevines

You betray us by the hour
in the mountain
of your success
the house of plenitude
of fullness
of deserts all made meaningful

Mouthed — not spoken

There, and the smallest words
mouthed — not spoken
in the language of flies
that lies before us
like a battleground
full of rats
and torn clothing
alive with night moaning

And the language of God
went awalking by the crystal fountain
saying "Water" saying "Grass"
saying "Trees"
then little words, like "Mouse"
and "Mosquito"

The rock is a very pure place
the womb of rock is very silent
in such a stony dance encoded
till the sound of God shall whisper "Roots"
till the sigh of God shall answer "Frost"
till a splinter in the eye of God
splits the expectant mountain

Jealous children

These episodes
and the rain beats the city flat
the neon city
its accumulated ghosts
stratigraphies of loneliness
and strangers in the dull rooms of our fear

The house that moved
to the tone of laughter
where angels steadfastly met us
held us in their gaze

the circle
and the span of fear
how you caused us laughter
move sweetly as the wind
that is about us

The descent of fear
this earthly habitation
this garden
where desire found you wanting
your spirit moves with the trees
in the semblance of that wind

and now we know
the places we depicted on our maps
and youthfully
you've spoken to us

Voices between these poles of dream
and all the words we know
are coming back
like jealous children

we are thankful then
for the way our tongues
bore us on the flood of silence
but bitter between your teeth
that sentence
and it's so full of muttering

As the cold winds bite

And Voice,
that spirit that you see — speak of
as dust — present to me

at home within the darkness
no knowledge quite like this
Oh little ghost of dream
where will I find you?

and all these ways
light is most unkind to us
as here indeed you feel it
cold as wind's bite
upon your plasmic corporality

You faded like the dancers
and all you told us then
and all we could believe

Bombastic Empires

How,
Father of silences
farmer of all the white spaces
that lie, and feed upon language,

Redeem our vocabularies
for we are caught
within the bombastic empires
of haughty planets
crowned and bound by fire.

The edge, the rinde, the frontier
belong to us interminably
poor farmland — sparse pasture
fen country of disturbing dreams

and that dark shape that sits
upon your tongue, our familiar
the crouching word
whispering that energetic phrase
becoming nightfall
as proud as winter is
with its array of favorite teeth
frozen ground
and fields of ice crystals

Within this other sphere
these fragmentary times
touch told us
taste marked its colours
and the sound of celestial telephones
burnt bright holes in the dome of night

and thus the world became
heaven's cold wonderland

By the dark wall

Old heros then
within the glove of battles

this world
where the past and the future
find themselves beneath our finger nails
we have found so much surprise
by the dark wall
and that town
rich with the uses of your imagination
Flowers fell here, indeed
roses within the labyrinths of the sea

You turn the tides on us
time beat us
with its little sticks
bearing the remembrance
of fish traps
and the people you know
are unable to distill the sense of it
the motion of time, vomit of old stones
and stories where ghosts visit
and silences contain you like a seed

Deriving purposes from nonsense

Deriving purposes from nonsense
the clock beat itself
into a mockery of time

Imagine the perplexity of sunflowers
and then how — somewhere else
the ghost of history
is busy writing up, for you
a humorous obituary

Believe you me
time has occupied us
like an invading army
or a plague of snails
within the muddy landscape
of our memory

The inevitable coital mystery

Houses of darkness
and all the witticism of the sea
cruising jelly fish, rocks matted with sea-wrack
curled and waved by the rising waters
floors of bitter carpets
rushes and crumpled cigarets
dancefloors that celebrate the trap of love
the inevitable coital mystery
enacted on this wood
and all the world of little fish
among the barnacles

Discover the lie in everything
old men moving with the brutal wind
that sweeps them up to heaven
in the precincts of their precarious vice

Mouths
drinking each other's breath
I hold you in the soul,
like lemonade

You mystify me
with your providence
I will untie the dark
like a sack full of butterflies

Melons for meloncholy

Have I forgotten to remember you?
you pleasant spirit
little dusty creature
small toothed animal
inhabiter of all the forests undersea
kelp angel
urchin lover
nibbler of the precious flesh
of paddling children

how far we reach a word
collectively we seem
it's our surprise
these obvious moments
when our informal darkness
clambered up and caught the moon

but I say "Love"
and my palace of words
all falls down
just like the nursery rime
food for thought
melons for meloncholy
and herrings for the deaf

I'll go down to the Sally Ann

It is impossible to write anything important
I've been to a death
and you ask me for some message
but there was no message
only Death

So now I'm busy
thinking up a message
to hand to you

an eternal truth
that you will take and set
like a gaudy sacred jewel
but I tell you once again
there was no message

all I can say
in that ordinary apartment
there suddenly was an absence

Yes, I've been around
when absence came into the world
when time stopped
and time went on
and all my illusions then became
as they are — illusions

and now you see me
sitting scribbling in this cafe
naked as a little baby

so I tell you
I'll go down to the Sally Ann
pick out another suit of clothes
to mock myself in last years fashions

for, I tell you, I've seen Death
it was a strong wind
blew all my clothes away

The fox in the trap

"And You" I say
and how do we speak to the Dead?
what elevated language can we use?
the ordinary things
of touch and sight
and busyness

have lost their relevance
and you have now become
unchangeable
but this language that we use
is very fickle
very down to earth
ordinary
and mutable

and now you are now
none of these

So I must find a language
then I can talk to you

And even then
you have become
the spirit's person

I mean
I'll wear you like a scar

How fast words left us
free of it all
no longer making little expeditions
into language

very full of your animal desire

and then we reasonably
chewed on the idea
of making history into the world again
so bitter with it

the fox in the trap
that chewed her leg off
and so escaped

Towards the ocean where the snakes are hidden

Well the world as we know it
this precious place
where time has spun us
like the disease we watched
consume all the bread
and the peanut butter

What have you seen
beyond us?
Beyond the edge of the beach
beyond the hills
and the last houses
beyond the wheatfields
and the market gardens
beyond supper
and winter
the mudbank
the outfall
and the silted up canal
beyond bridges of brickwork
and the chainlinked fences
the concrete culverts
and the fields
eaten by butterflies
and towards the ocean
where the snakes lie hidden
the little fish
and the porcupines
beyond Heaven and Earth
Hell and that other garden
the marriageable tide
and the ocean of suffering
and the land that sank under
all those depths of water
where in stormy weather
you can hear the churchbells ringing

beyond all these places we have been
where now you travel on beyond us
and in the dark
you hear these voices calling

We spin our tires

And the fire that burnt us all away
You went to the fire
I did not imagine that
and the fire takes us all
and hides us
under the lip of flame

And in the mouths of this country
Death has laid the wheatfields down
and now in the thick mud
we are unable
to move either foreward of backward
as we spin our tires
digging ourselves in to the axels

and then beneath our last historic waterfall
you told us
as you waited, watched
saw us in our accompanying darkness

How much you had hoped
we'll never know
and the truth of the matter is
it's a foolish business all this surviving
you might have said: how we belong to silence
It has sealed us

Aug'87

Evidence
for Jane

We watch it
 like this is
  of the sea
  of the city
caught a ferry
 went back to his wife
 his mother
  to the old country
he went back to work
 he went beyond us
  he went away on a bus
  on a train
  on a ferry
  on a plane.
He jumped in a canoe
 he jumped on a horse
  he jumped onto a balloon
  he jumped out
   and parachuted slowly to the earth
   he jumped into the water
   and swam to the island
    and lay panting on the beach
    he jumped into the pool
    and swam two lengths
    underwater
     he went into the sauna
He took a ship
he went away
he was here today
but he went away
and that is where he is
away.
He came in a cab
 no, he came on a camel
  he came again in a bathtub
  he came in bed

115

But he went
  he went on the subway
   he went on the elevator
    in the library
     he went between the pages of that book
     he went after the last semi-colon
      in that paragraf
      halfway down the third page
he went to sea
  he went to the zoo
   he looked at the rhinoceros
   he looked at the mating frogs
   he looked at the shark
    with its sharp mouth
    open

He kept a sharp lookout for pickpockets
  he kept a sharp look out
for children on bicycles riding without lights
  he kept a sharp look out
for lovers in the long grass

he kept a sharp look out
       for pennies in the gutter
       for knives and things like that
       for razorblades and mowers
       and movers

Here he was in this coffee shop
  here is his dirty cup
  here he was, in this lineup
   at the employment exchange
   at the courthouse
   on the dole
here he was, in this picture
  in the line up at the soup kitchen
  here he is
   in this old fotograf
   with his children on his knee

and others behind him
 their faces in shadow
  you can see the camera shake
   and the half moon of thumb across the lens
but yet it's the best we have of him.

Here he is beside the sea
 with his pants rolled up
  above the knee
   digging clams
    with his little boy
Here he is with his old dog
licking his face
 as he tries to push it
  away
and here, you see, in this picture that he took
 the old car that got him there and back
  so many times
   and finally split its gut
    or blew a rod
     or just died, or so

and here's one of his women
 standing by the door of the old car
  and here's another of his women
   whole stacks of pictures of different ladies
    all standing in the same awkward manner
     as he says, "Smile please"
      and pulls their faces
       into his camera
      and sticks them on his film
       all those ladies

Look!
This one bore him
 a couple of sons
  this one went with him
   to continental movies
    all black and white

117

they'd talk for hours at the expresso bar
 she'd kiss him quick at the door
and here is the lady
 he'd dream about
  but never got much further than
   pointing his camera at

"luckless with ladies, love shy" he'd say

and here are more ladies
 this was his mother
  here she is crying
   by the garden gate
    he went away

here is his sister
 here are the words he cannot say
  and here
   with her long hair
in the low evening sun one day
 just at the edge of the sea

he jumped on a train
 he jumped on a boat
  he jumped on a bus
   he jumped on the train, another train
they bore him swiftly away
 this is the picture of the lady
  who bore him two daughters and a son
   and went away

here is the picture
 of someone elses son
  who got his name
   like a broken toy

and here is the distinct advantage
 which he can not see
  here is the manner of speaking

he came with
 here is his accent
  as he talks about the weather

  and his happiness
   planting radishes
    in his scruffy garden

here are his feet
 shuffling through the snow
and his ears always hearing things
flapping about like birds
here is the way he wanted to be
 and here is the thing he became
and here is the picture of him going
 just before he went away

   —1981

Glossary

for Connie Fife

Anarchy — a political system based on individual responsibility rather than force. A world in which all things are possible, in which all people are respected equally, the Land of Cockayne, the Big Rock Candy Mountain.

Anglo Saxon — a vigorous, highly inflected, beautiful but obscure and sometimes obscene germanic language, brutally repressed after 1066 ad

Art — the gift that the poor give to the rich. What we venerate, or pretend to venerate. The ultimate in conspicuous consumption, the pillage of ancient tombs. Public culture reduced to private property.

Babel, Tower of — built by Nimrod, annoying God who, to spite him made everyone speak a different language, thereby bringing construction to a halt, making foreign travel more interesting and mentally stimulating. The Biblical theory of the Evolution of Languages. (see *Word, Tongue*)

Bad Poetry — the poetry we'd like to have written, but didn't dare to. Poetry that oversteps the bounds of good taste.

Binding — from the Anglo Saxon, Bindan — to tie together. The habit of tying books together with linen thread originated with the Copts at Alexandria, where they maintained a famous library.

Binding, Perfect — making "Books" by temporally fastening the pages together with glue, creating a marketable commodity, but most imperfect.

Binding, Sewn — making books by sewing the pages together in "Gatherings", "Booklets" or "Signatures", using linen thread. The traditional form of binding, dating back to Classical times.

Body — the Garden of Delights. See *Flesh*.

Book — a discrete work of literature, complete within itself, preferably tied together with linen thread.

Broadsheet — a sheet printed on both sides, laid out in such a way that when it is folded it will make a booklet, the pages appearing in the right order, often sold around the streets by unlicenced peddlars or chapmen in the early days of printing.

Broadside — the simultaneous firing of all the guns on one side of a Man of War in a naval battle. Often a political tract printed as a poster, or a ballard commemorating a notable execution, sold by a chapman. A poem printed, usually by letter- press on a single unfolded sheet of paper.

Canada Council — the Canadian system of funding the Arts, though generally worthy, not beyond criticism, not greatly loved by artists, under constant attack by governments, and the self proclaimed watch dogs of the public purse and public morality. See *Hierarchy*.

Chapbook — a book or pamphlet sold cheaply by chapmen or peddlers, a scurrilous occupation pursued by lowbows since the introduction of printing. literature of the lower classes, beneath the dignity of scholastics.

Chap — from Anglo Saxon *Ceop* to barter or swap

Cockayne, Land of — the land of Eternal Spring, eternal plenty, the Garden of Delight, the Luddites' Heaven on Earth where the noise of the machine will be stilled.

Competition — The reduction or raising of the the culture of poetry to the level of an agricultural show. See *Hereford*.

Copyright — the barbed wire of literature upon the prairie of the imagination.

Correct Thinking — the idea that the products of the imagination should be bought and sold in the market place.

Critic, Jury, Canada Council — hierarchies set up to promote correct thinking among artists.

Creative Writing — a short cut to poetry (perhaps)

Culture — the living spark, the active ingredient in beer, yogurt, bread, society. The representation of what we do; who we are; how we survive.

The web and the woof of human activity, a very public thing. Like 'Art' but without the money.

Day Job — wot u gotta do, to keep *Body* and *Soul* together (q.v.). See *Job*.

Devil — God on a bad day. Blake's companion when he read the Bible. God, when she needed take an unpopular action, called by the insurance industry 'an act of God'. A little voice that tries to lead us from the stony paths of righteousness into the leafy forests of delight. A a force for evil rendered obsolescent by modern technology who finds work for idle hands. See *Job*.

Ear — a suitable gift for ones loved one, often requested in loan by unscrupulous politicians. The orifice in which sweet poetry resounds.

Editor — the rank above Poet in the hierarchy of literature. A willing ear, sympathetic critic, friend indeed, for prose writers.

Flesh — our feeling substance, which, with the World and the Devil, forms the inferior trinity. See *Devil*.

Gaia Hypothesis — the hypothesis that the processes of life originally shaped, and continue to control our physical environment. The Unified Field Theory of Life.

God — Odin or Loki, Zeus or Kali, or the guy or gal that art in heaven (see *Art*). The One Reality, the Ultimate Abstraction, the Great Unknown, the unnamable way, the black hole at the centre of the universe.

Goddess — similar to God (q.v.) but with superior intellect, understanding, compassion and beauty, mixed with delicious cruelty.

He, his, him — the poet in male manifestation. See *She, Her; Ho, Hor.*

Hierarchy — the rule by a priesthood, where the guy at the top talks with God and passes the Word and opinions of God down to *Hoi Poloi*, which is Greek for The People. Anathema to culture, a disease of civilization.

History — interesting times, a nightmare, one of the raw materials of poetry. See *Herecleitus*.

Ho, hor — a unisex pronoun that the language lacks, invented by the writer as necessity is the mother of invention.

Human Soul — a metaphysical organism resembling a bird, that sings in Heaven, or roasts in Hell. See Egyptian and Tibetan Books of the Dead, the Prose Edda etc.

Job — the victim of a friendly wager between *God* (q.v.) and the *Devil* (q.v.)

Language — See *Babel*

League — ½ a League, ½ a League onwards. (Tennyson)

Letterpress — printing using raised metal type, in a technique that has evolved since the introduction of printing in the West by Guttenberg and friends, invented in Korea several centuries previously for the printing of religious texts. The traditional and time-honoured way of printing.

Money, Moolah — the Only Reality, the Ultimate Abstraction. A truely metaphysical concept. See 'God.' To those that have shall be given from those that have not shall be taken away even what they have.

Negative Capability — Poets' got it, that's why they die young, even though they're immortal, and why they never write good poetry till after they're good and dead.

Poem — a work of art employing the vagaries of language. See *Art, Language*.

Poet — a dancer in the dance of language. A poor numbskull cursed with Negative Capability.

Poetaster — a young fellow who tastes poetry, and spits it out.

Poetess — a poet in communication with the Goddess. The last great poetess was Dame Edith Sitwell, and there'll never be another one like her.

Poetic, Poetique — an aesthetic affectation.

Poetic license — a right and an obligation awarded you when your imagination first wrestles with language in loving embrace. A sort of marriage license. An oath of poverty. See the Canada Tax Guide.

Poetry — a playful organization of speech sounds, and (sometimes hidden) meanings.

Poetry Slam — the low art of poetry raised to the heights of the NHL.

Poverty — the natural environment of poets. See *Gaia Hypothesis.*

Plato — a Greek philosopher of fascistic leanings.

Publish — getting your work on the shelves of bookstores.

Publisher — the guy you hope has money to bet on your excellence.

Right — to set in order, to right a boat, to right a wrong, to preserve the status quo, see RCMP. Perhaps poems sometimes need a little righting, but a poem can never be quite right, more likely to be left, as in 'left out in the cold'.

Rite — a religious or spiritual act. Rites tend to involve spells.

Ryt — to fashion a poem, navigate between the banks of illogicality and irony. To discover beauty in the human predicament. See wright, write.

Schadenfreud — (German) joy of disgrace, usually of others, sometimes of oneself.

Self publishing — the rite of the poet, as conferred by poetic licence.

She, her — the poet in female manifestation.

Spell — a magical incantation to summon spirits up from the Earth, or down from the Heavens. You gotta do it rite, or you'll get something you didn't bargain for.

Tongue — "the limb that has no bone that women love" Webster '*Duchess of Malfi*' q.v.

Unacknowledged legislators — poets, they write the only laws that bear any relationship to Justice, but are not blindfolded and are therefore ignored.

Voice — the prime and ancient organ of poetry, unfortunately less mighty than the sword, being situated above the neck, but of longer reach, being born upon the air and subject to the wonderful effects of echo.

Word — "and the word became flesh..." See *Flesh*.

Wright — to fashion with great skill and artifice, a shipwright, wheelwright, a playwright, to wright poem.

Write — the act of putting verbal sounds in visual form, of drawing language on a receptive suface as in calligraphy.

Zine — an instantaneous publication from the dark side of the culture, printed by photo copying, paid for with borrowed pennies, spreading with the grass roots across N. America. Pure Punk. The Word once more becoming flesh. The crabgrass of literature. See Chapbook, also Blake: *Marriage of Heaven and Hell*.

All poets are invited to use, contradict, add to, transmit, copy, etc. this glossary in any way they wish. Not protected by barbed wire.

Poitry Man
There wos this poitry man
his name wos Jesus
but they dun him in
an mony another too

He wos a poor man
just left his foot prints
for you to find
where he walked
this tired erth
an a few words
he left behind
for our misquotation

an as I say
he aint the only won
wot been dun in
for poitry .